This Next Tenderness

Also by Ellen Steinbaum

Afterwords
Container Gardening
Brightness Falls

This Next Tenderness

Poems by Ellen Steinbaum

CW Books

*For John and Brenda —
with thanks and
good wishes —
Ellen Steinbaum*

Published by CW Books

P.O. Box 541106

Cincinnati, OH 45254-1106

ISBN: 978-1-62549-267-8

Poetry Editor: Kevin Walzer

Business Editor: Lori Jareo

Visit us on the web at www.readcwbooks.com

Again for Jim

and for our family of

Archers

Bakers

Dalsimers

Redleners

Russells

"Everything tender and melancholy—as life is sometimes, just for one moment."

Jean Rhys, *Good Morning, Midnight*

Contents

II. Still Life

I. Small Present

Snowdrops in January

A few mild days and they are pushing up,
white petals drooped in modest triumph,
open to the gift.

"Rushing the season," my mother called it,
shook her head at someone's shed coat
or short sleeves.

"We won't have snowdrops in the spring,"
I worry. "But," he says,
"we have them now."

Esse / Habere

The second thing is this: to have.
We arrive and close our fists on
stone and feather
this, not that
in passion or
in casual reaching out
and pocketing.

This is our history: a line from
first picked-up twig through
painted curling lemon rind to
heaped-up things lost into drawers
still stiff with the fading
shine of our attention.

What can we know as well as
a bowl presented for our
polished gaze beyond
its temporary owner and
the painter skilled with
curve and light?

Only Connecting

I log on and see two friends announce their marriage.
They've been together decades, share a grandchild:
I have made assumptions I must now revise—
together all these years unwed? I cheer their
non-convention, wonder why they've married now.
And then I see her at the gym, offer congrats and she,
embarrassed, says she was filling in her profile and
it turned, somehow, into news. Updates from him
seem to reflect a new sanctity, a new appreciation
for what they had done years before. So I send him
congratulations and am prompted, "send a gift" and
where it's usually the Starbucks card, now, inexplicably,
I'm urged to send him collar stays, something I wouldn't
have thought of on my own, thank you, because,
though I am fond of him, I've never thought to send him
gifts and collars stays would hardly be my choice
since I've seen him only wearing open-collared shirts
(and now it sounds as if I've noticed too much and
that's a little awkward, him with that newly-married status)
and does anyone buy collar stays as gifts these days?
I see they're sold at Tiffany "for the man of distinction,"
in silver, monogrammed, but "this item is no longer available"
so it seems that even Tiffany has seen the writing on the wall
which is sometimes news and sometimes just a statement
that things continue as they are.

for KA and RH

Recorded History

Rising out of the bath water
the familiar knees
show two faint scars
from the bicycle errand
when I was eight or maybe ten,
and, from the same fall, scars
inside left elbow, on heel of right hand,
now so faint no one else would notice
but I know where to search,
remember sitting, shaky,
at the drugstore counter,
patting small blood with napkin,
sipping water, saying yes,
I was all right, then peddling home
slowly, milk and bread intact
and though I know our cells replace themselves,
replicate and reproduce until we're new,
the scars remain all these years later,
visible as cave paintings
if you know where to look.

Good Day Sir or Madam

Mrs. Caro Hu says Hello,
I know I have never met you,
but my mind instincts me to
do this. I believe everything
happens for a reason. People
change so you can learn to let go.
Things go wrong so you can
appreciate them when they're right.

I am a dying woman
who has decided to donate
what I have to you.
For charitable goals.

Kindly contact my lawyer
through this email or on
his private line if you are
interested in carrying out this
task. I will not be available.
He can arrange the release
of funds to you ($10,500,000.00)
Thank you and God bless you.
Keep this confidential because
of the 7.01% tax on the funds.

I have no children. Please forget
about my family members. It is a
long story.

Sleeves

My friend is shopping for a dress,
"with sleeves," she says, not
happily. I understand. The quest
may not end in success: it's hard
to find that sweet forgiveness
for shortcomings of the flesh.

Where are the graceful
dolman, gentle cap,
and flirty flutter? Long
sleeves now are inked
in blue while our blue
lines, by contrast, are
just what we'd hide away.
Best draw a tender veil
over ravelled skin, let limbs
experienced in the daily
sacraments repose
in privacy.

This flesh is decorous: no
casual glimpse without
admission paid. Novels
are written here, worldly
as pears in varnished still life
gone just past ripe and
browning at the edge.

If invited, look at it in awe.
Gasp in wonder as if at
giant redwoods whose circles
count out Tang, Ming, Columbus,
rockets to the moon. We, too,
have stood fast through fickle years

and we have nothing up our sleeves
but this slight human covering,
no less, we're told, than stardust.

for SHD

It starts like tenderness

the helping hand cupping the elbow
that we shake off as if we didn't notice,
as if we felt no sting.

The children—adults now, middle-aged—
take bundles from our hands,
solicitous in unburdening, and—
like us—calibrating, sounding for decay.

Before their visits we clear the house
of the crimes of expired cereal, aspirin;
cut back the looming shrubs
that shroud the houses of the old.

In restaurants we watch
the slow, unsteady passage
to nearby tables, measure ourselves
against the faltering before us.

A Small Prayer of Healing

Peace may not be granted,
may not drop into our open hands,
may be withheld by accident of time or place.
Weeping may tarry even in the morning and
there may be pulsing borders, words like swords.

What, then, is given?
Our every breath
spreads outward:
We must do what we can.

looking through the bone

after Georgia O'Keeffe

look here
through this
don't try to see
the whole sky or
every cloud

make this your eye
sun-bleached white
against blue
blue showing through
white

the bone
imperious
commanding
        look here
        look only here
        only now
        blot out the rest

not too much
only this one bit of blue
this piece of cloud
only this
        less
        less

Covert Negotiations

Assumptions have been made;
this has been the case for years:
clothes bought to fit your size and shape,
nails filed and whiskers shaved
as if you owned them,
a conceit of hardiness,
of strength that you could count on
and meanwhile (*meanwhile*, that
insidious betrayer) you were the host
to secrets: a bargain taking place
without your knowledge or consent.

for TBS

A Later Appointment Has Been Scheduled

The sweat-wet drench of reprieve:
it will not be this and not
this day, though it will be
one this and one day but not
this exact wolf circling
hungry-eyed and patient,
hungry-eyed, patient.

Carrying the Mark

We have something in common, he says,
and I know he is saying he can see it—
the shadowy mark just above my shoulder,
dark smudge on my doorpost, sign
of damage I can nearly always hide.

They see it, though, the ones
who carry paled or livid
evidence of their own,
the ones for whom the scar
marks me as safe.

Not the untouched,
unscathed, whole—
they would not be chosen
to hear the damage report

Snow effect

"I've always wanted to see snow," my cousin Eliana writes
from Rio where my great-grandmother's sister went instead of
Philadelphia. Here it is the usual-- tree limbs bent
with the weight, cartoon shape cars and gnome caps
on the garden lights. Inside light glares blinding bright
at the windows carving deeper lines on my face, soft-focusing
the paintings in the hall beneath the muffled skylights. Eliana
sees the news reports, the emptied supermarket shelves
(though I must tell her that here in a fortunate place, my
pre-storm rush to shop involved a recipe requiring thyme and
fennel and the man behind me in the line bought kumquats
and heavy cream). Technically she saw snow once:
on a train leaving Chicago someone pointed to the window
at light flurries in the sunlight, but they were gone in seconds;
she has never seen this kind, that's shoveled, marked in inches,
though it's in our Russian shtetl DNA. She says in Rio it is 93—
a little cooler than the day before--and it is Carnival. She sends me
links to sambas, tells me to click where it says "skip this ad" in
Portuguese. And I am listening to sambas when the e-mail comes
from my friend Jack, who died two weeks ago. Of course they'd
use his e-mail, where all his grouped addresses are, but
it was startling to see his name there on the announcement
that the memorial would be postponed a day because of snow.

Day at the Circus

In the grainy picture the tiger looks
a little bored while the boy,
his hand placed lightly on her back,
seems poised to leap away if she
should make a move. The Russian parents
love this souvenir: between the acts
the lions, monkeys, bears are props
for children's photographs. There can be
accidents, of course, the story says—
a toddler bitten hard enough to break his skull,
a schoolgirl who now wears a leopard scar.
One child holds back, is allowed to go,
instead, for cotton candy; another whispers,
"Do you think she is full?" while sitting warily
beside the lion. The circus owner reassures,
pockets the extra cash and shrugs, says risk
is everywhere in life.

Available for Download: Freud's Interpretation of Dreams

now playing in our heads
the onion peels of costumed thought and
wish, the fleeting and the burned-in constant,
fantastical, forbidden, and mundane, into the
swirls and circlings of our shrouded selves
fantastical, forbidden, and mundane, into the
wish, the fleeting and the burned-in constant
the onion peels of costumed thought and
now playing in our heads

Here

I

Overnight snow on branches
mirrored light
lazy flakes floating to ground:

this is the world we never want
to leave, though it's constantly working
to discard us—mere fingernail clipping,
onion skin.

Our ancestors drew flat maps
edged with hazards—dragons with fierce teeth
and claws dug into the nothing who watch
for our slip from the precarious surface.

Most often, though, we do not slide,
do not fall swiftly, cleanly; no, we snag,
we catch, hang—burning—until we pray
to fall into the open jaws.

II

The fantasy is that one day
no more than simply frail
we will lie down
in our soft bed,
hold hands
and sleep
no unraveling
no one taking
car keys from our hands
or watching over every
step and mouthful
no being left
or overstaying
just departure
bon voyage
tender as the pleated skin
inside our elbows

III.

It seems it was just fable—
the maps never really said,
 "hic sunt dracones,"
though fearsome dragons
were pictured, also
elephants, serpents, scorpions,
and "here lions abound"
(*abound!*) was written, practically inviting
frolicking in the face of certain doom—
but only fable, never on the maps
though warning nonetheless
of something waiting
at the unimagined edge,
though we know where
the dragons really are.

Celebrating the Fourth

This is privilege: to walk the beach
then climb weathered steps to
perfect lawn and sunwarmed pool.

This is good fortune: set the table
for fifteen while listening to music,
spreading newspapers—it will be

messy—lobsters set on every plate,
corn piled high, and good
white wine on ice, clouds pinking as we watch.

Our friend has leaned his crutches up against
the wall. We are careful with him, know he is fragile.

In Our Image

From two rooms away the sound is startling:
the printer, unattended, is cleaning itself,
grooming, like a cat, but with a notice-me noise
the way our newest musical contraption,
wakes us with burbled clearing of its throat.

Even when we aren't there, want nothing from them,
our inventions yearn to serve, call out to us and
want attention—*do not forget us*, they say,
when you sleep, dream about us,
keep us close, keep needing us.

Small Present

Was it a joke, this thought that, being fortunate
enough to want for nothing, only time,
we'd buy ourselves this trifling gift, replacement for
the humble kitchen gadget, finger-smeared and
taped together, that offered helpful information?
Just as I am noting the anniversary moment of
the moment and am looking at photographs of our
years-younger selves where no child yet
is old enough to drive and where the youngest
is not yet an older brother, I see it on the table:
shiny new and in a package promising
a "loud alarm," this fresh addition
ready to tick off our minutes, seconds,
let us know when time is up.

Fright

Each day comes with new undoing
imperceptible, relentless.
This is not the month called cruel, but
October, too, keeps its terrors sharp:
it is the season of subtraction.

Time to decide what horror, what disgust
to face down, what to turn into a joke.
In the early darkened streets walks
the parade of fears—gleefully disguised
daily selves, innocent bedsheet ghosts
of years past morphed into zombies dripping gore,
imagined monsters that skirt the edge of truth.

And here, two toddlers—baby faces recast
into a laughingstock of age, bewigged with grey
and fitted out with glasses, cut-down canes—
parade as almost us. We are disguises now, a source
of public farce. This is not savage mocking,
just good-natured fun, that lays bare our unraveling,
our holding on as friends succumb and our own powers
grow more fragile day by day. We laugh with them,
allow them not to see how the colorful winding-down
in golden light and apple-scented air
holds what is waiting to be lost.

Solitaire

"Patience" it's called in Victorian novels where
the heroine sits prettily at a small table near the fire,
fingering the cards and pretending to ignore the suitor
making shy, distracted talk across the room.

On screen the cards fly at a finger jab and winning
is just a moment's sour hesitation before
the joyless play starts again and though we have
little interest and no patience, we cannot seem to

stop, even without the satisfying shuffle sound
or chance to see the card we hoped for
would be turned up next. We're rehearsing
desolation, grimly rushing to new game, new game,

heads down as if we're yoked
and have a field ahead to plow.

The shiva rice pudding

was the only one I ever made
that turned out wrong—watery
beneath the cinnamon-sugar topping.
And I forgot the raisins. She
made it year after year in the old red
wedding gift baking dish, then
in the new red baking dish bought
after the first one broke.

It's always more or less about the food—
the chicken soup, the casseroles, and, yes,
rice pudding, her mother's recipe.
Still, what else can we do but bring out these
pale reminders year after year and set out plates?

Lady/Tiger

We were wrong:
the operative word
it turns out
was
and.

When push
comes to shove
you have to
have it
both ways.

This has always
been the case.

instructions for shelling peas

if you're in a hurry
cut up summer squash instead
snip the tips of green beans
take your sharpest knife and
slice tomatoes
don't make peas

peas slow you down
urge you outside
to a wicker chair or
porch swing
to air so heavy
sunshine so bright
that coming back inside
you will squint

do not shell peas while
you stand at a counter
listening to news
stripping the pods
to sounds of gunfire or politics
impatient while the meager mass
edges upward in a measuring cup

think about your childhood
shelling peas as your grandmother
told you stories or as you
giggled with your sister
if you do not have these memories
if you do not have a sister
you can make them up
but don't distract yourself completely
pay attention to the peas

eat some right away
from the metal bowl on your lap
cool against your bare legs
squeeze every pod
and when it opens
be charmed each time

II. Still Life

Pronk

Take this in—the glowing fullness,
saturated reds and blues,
velvet and marble,
the rare and precious.

Consider the world inside each frame—
fat globes of grapes enormous, perfect;
wet slit of coral-colored melon;
hams and lobsters; lemon rind curled

off the table's thick draped edge;
unblemished flowers out of season;
gleaming chargers tipped under the weight
of oysters nearly slipping from

their shells. The bounty astounds,
spills out its lesson at your feet:
not the heaped-up treasure, no,
but the fearless savoring.

Love Letter to Women I Don't Know

I.
They were beautiful, despite frailties and
the damages of time—a curving back,
a spreading middle—beautiful: two friends out
on a shopping trip together who briefly
shared their companionship with me,
trading opinions as we tried on clothes
in the common dressing room
where, though they were not
all that far past my age,
I could see them see
that I still could
wear a sleeveless dress.

II.
In MOMA's second floor cafe
at the counter we sit side by side
looking out at West 53rd Street.
On my right a woman cuts her child's
grilled cheese sandwich and
nibbles at the crusts he leaves
untouched. The woman on my left
looks elegant in that midtown
Manhattan way, dressed in
her uniform of black with
interesting earrings, bangle bracelet,
and a scarf. She looks relaxed,
eats slowly through three courses,
ending with an ice cream cone.

III.
In National's Terminal C, she is waiting
for a traveler and, at Mayorga Coffee, I
watch her watch the arrivals. She is small;
wears cropped pants, tee shirt, orange shoes;
has nicely-cut gray hair. She looks sturdy, capable,
yet somehow fragile, somehow guarded against hurt
and I feel protective, hope the face she seeks
will light to see her. No, please not that man, paunchy
and in silly shorts, not any of those blank-faced travelers
rushing past, please no one in a baseball cap. I watch
her want and then the recognition of, perhaps, a daughter.
They do not hug or talk, just trade small smiles and walk
in matching strides toward baggage claim and
I can only hope the visit works out well.

Good morning/Sorry

With breakfast coffee I take in pages full of news
that tinge my steaming sips with minor salt—
small sidewalk rudenesses—luggage wheel run over
foot, pointing arm outstretched into cheek—and
not one "I'm sorry." Not like Naghma's father
who is, yes, sorry that she, at six, must marry
as payment for his debt. He is sorry but what can he do—
money was needed for firewood, medicine. "Everyone
gives away their child," he says. Naghma does not know
yet and he does what he can to make her happy
this, her final year at home. Soon she will not
go to school—the teenaged groom-to-be prefers that—
and his parents, too, prefer it and are sorry.
She stands photographed in mud-caked boots, red skirt,
and patterned head scarf, twice destined for bad luck:
born a girl and born into long war. She likes to sing. Her name
means melody. But that story was months ago. Most likely
she is married now. Today's news has a photograph
of men in another far-off place lined up in wedding clothes,
each with a small girl dressed in white.

Enough

It used to be enough—remember?
"Enough already" we would say or maybe,
nodding, "enough said" or "that's enough"
to stop a flow of grating noise or pouring drink.
Enough...just right... a satisfactory amount.
But more and more
enough is not enough.
Enough is disappointing,
too scant to fill our rented storerooms
and our movie popcorn tubs.
We need sandwiches too tall to eat,
profits higher than last year's,
and everything more than what it was:
No one has enough to live on anymore.

Another News Story on the Web

In this story every detail is fantastical:
the Australian town called Wagga Wagga,
the floodwaters rolling up on shore
chasing tiny uncountable spiders
to higher ground. That's what it says,
"uncountable spiders," though we know that,
given time, they could be counted.
And then you see the picture of the field,
the trees, the gauzy dog and, no, that isn't snow
but the heavy webs of the uncounted spiders.
Who can explain these things? Yet you can
click the link and see how flooding
made spiders climb, as well, into Pakistani trees
which, although different from
the Wagga Wagga trees are likewise
veiled by evidence of spiders spinning
desperate rescue, counting only on themselves.

Another Small Prayer of Healing

The blessings come
into our lives,
pile up around us
as they have since
the wilderness.

Cities wait to be rebuilt.
What we are given,
what we can give
all the same gift:
worlds wait to be repaired.

One Percent Milk

If this is the privileged milk,
the you-can never-be-too-thin-or-too-
rich milk, then what percentage is
the milk of human kindness or
mother's milk here in the land of
milk and honey, here where privilege
is white as milk and where we
shouldn't cry if it's spilt?

Snap Trap

"Snap trap" was his recommendation
after a glance at the mouse droppings
under my kitchen sink. I refused,
said give me something else so I
won't have to see the deaths, and
he did and that was that.

But "snap trap"stayed with me like an earworm tune,
like "it's a small world after all" like
"who let the dogs out woof woofwoof woofwoof."
The spoken words, though harsh, are somehow
satisfying, and I say it once again to feel how neatly
the timid \a\ as in apple feels matched with the crisp
mouthfeel of the consonants, the way the lips shut
briskly over the p's. Snap. Trap. Snap trap. No nonsense
in those words, no wiggle room, no chance for appeal.

The jaws snap shut on the words the way a trap's
would have on a mouse, the way the black and white cat's
did on the rabbit it carried through my friend's garden
while she and I drank lemonade. Snap trap, I thought
when I saw that cat and the limp form hanging
from its mouth. Snap trap, I thought, with regret
for the rabbit, though none for the mouse,
and the words still tasty in my mouth.

If in that Room

written in Emily Dickinson's bedroom

The door doesn't close completely.
Was it always like this,
the chores following you up the stairs
their tapping soft, insistent, and you

trying to shut out even
the seduction of the garden
seeping through the crack
into your silence?

I have come in homage,
to look for your presence
in the ghost-dress under glass,
the desktop barely bigger than a page.

Recluse, you were called,
like some shy spider, but I visualize,
instead, a hot impatience
as you turned the china knob,

pressed your back against the door,
grateful for the solidness of wood,
even slightly open—the door,
yes, the important thing.

primitive

bison se lechant de La Madeleine

stand here
in front of glass
begin with what was seen
put aside
the easy distancing
the smooth assumption
of progress

begin here with line incised
in slice of reindeer wood
this precise bison
tender membrane
of ear nostril eyelid
careful hair
the figure barely longer
than a finger
older than the pyramids

begin here with carved
curving tongue
how warm it is
how wet
stretched out in lazy
soothing of an itch
the creature pleasure
in the scratch the stretch the yawn
observed recorded
though we cannot know
by whom
who else was there
who watched

before there was blue

because they could not yet
grow the plants
could not yet grind the rock
make paint or dye
they did not need to say
they did not need a word

because they looked at sky
saw copper
sea wine-dark
in every language
blue came last

because they did not have
the photograph
from outer space

because they had no word for it
though it was everywhere
they did not see it
there was no word
though it was everywhere
there was no blue

Here is the question

and the time is getting late—
what is it you want
to believe?
Who do you want to be?
The one who says no?
The one who says
perhaps, the one
who says why not?

Yes, it is a burning word,
a brick someone could use
to build a wall. You must
lift it gently, take it from their hands
as you might take matches
from a child, carefully and
without anger or rushing,
with only tender heed
that they do no damage
with something that can burn.

The Dutch still life bouquets

were all illusion—
profusions
heedless of season—
tulips, poppies,
morning glory,
late summer roses:
those imagined gatherings
in one abundant moment,
every petal gleaming
against dark.

Havdalah (Before You Leave)

The separation is not one
of harsh walls and backs turned
against closed doors. No, it
is just the gentle turning
from this to that: each treasured,
each impossible without the other.

We are a people who see
the sacredness in separation,
inhale the melancholy scent
of moments come and gone,
turn from the tender regret
of flame offered up
into sweet darkness of wine,
to hallow what remains.

What have we been
but human with each other
in all our beauty and our flaws,
imperfect bridge between above, below?
We have mounded up the stores of days,
our births and deaths and daily breathing,
walked together on the narrow path
that trips us up, that opens out,
the path of hidden and revealed,
of what we take and what we give.

And after we have lived each others' lives,
walked in one another's footsteps,
what can separation be but illusion?
We are woven into a single fabric:
everywhere we are, it will float above
to shelter us,
wrap around

to comfort us,
spread out before us
for a banquet
where we continue to sit together.

for RF

Inventing Abstraction

Imagine how shocking it was at first.
Is it a woman? A mandolin?
Some hissed and some applauded.
What is new can be disturbing.

Is it a woman? A mandolin?
The mind tries to make meaning.
Some hissed and some applauded:
There is discomfort in uncertainty.

The mind tries to make meaning
Color conceals its possibilities
There is discomfort in uncertainty
There are things we have no words for

Color conceals its possibilities
Suddenly there is only pure creation
There are things we have no words for
Without a light source there is no shadow

Suddenly there is only pure creation
Some hissed and some applauded
Without a light source there is no shadow
Imagine how shocking it was at first.

Taken

I
Once the cat disappeared and
the man who picked up at
Animal Control said she
may have been taken by coyotes.

That's what he said, taken
by coyotes, and I wondered if he meant
that she—the cat—had found coyotes
particularly charming or that she
had been carried off by them—a trophy
or a houseguest.

II
We couldn't find his grave, my friend—
his widow on her first visit there—and I.
We thought we knew the spot and she had
a piece of paper with his new address—
the section, row, and plot. There should have been
a temporary marker but there was only
undifferentiated grass, no newer,
greener looking patch.

"It was the squirrels," the caretaker told us,
sounding apologetic. "I know it sounds strange,"
he said, "but the temporary plates are shiny and
get carried off by squirrels. There's one I've found and
put back four times already."

III
The cat returned, only a little worse
for the adventure which did not, it seemed,
involve coyotes after all. She lived only
another few weeks, almost got to 20—ancient
for a cat. The end, as it turned out, did not involve
coyotes either, although ever since I've found
something slightly pleasant in the thought of
being taken by coyotes.

IV
We never found the grave although we found
the general location. But all in all she was glad
not to have seen the very place, the shiny
marker on small grass; felt that, instead,
he could be anywhere, everywhere,

in clouds and trees and on the ground where
there were chipmunks, rabbits, and
the thieving squirrels and we
saw them all and were taken.

for CBM

Birthday on the Morningside Unit

The cake has yellow roses and a single green
candle. They wait in their seats—the one who
grabs the others' napkins; the one who fidgets,
gets distracted; and the birthday girl, who asks
if everyone's arrived and says, yes,
she wants the ice cream *and* the cake.
Prompted to sing, they manage most
of the words they've sung
since the days when their cheeks
were round and pink and their adoring
parents stood around the table, watching.

Berlin Philharmonic Concert 11/11/_ _18

Maybe she also sat mid-orchestra,
center—it could have happened—
also fingering a length of pearls,
as she waited for Mahler's Seventh,
settled into her plush seat,
reading the program and nodding
to nearby friends. It could have happened
on this same weighted date, a different year:
the houselights dimmed,
the conductor was applauded,
then the expectant hush,
the opening notes. And she,
the woman I imagine, could have
willed herself into the flood of sound
that drowned out the rest.

in the hall of remarkable women

see here is the one who turned back the sea
the one whose hand smoothed oceans
the one who sang the song
here the one who tricked the king
and freed the people
the one who gathered multitudes
taught the animals to speak
sang rocks and trees into existence
poured sustenance
from an earthenware pitcher
this is the one who resolute
spoke back to tide and wind
the one who covered sand with water

still life

how to explain the pull of it
Dreher painting day after day
decades of days
the glass the table the blank white wall
the glass the table the blank white wall

Morandi grouping regrouping
his vases bowls tall-necked bottles
calibrating the rhythm of their shadows
muted colors
solid shapes

Coorte placed the day's objects
on the one stone ledge
with its one slim seam
bundle of fat asparagus
translucent gooseberries
lush medlars
peaches
row of shells

both our fathers as late-life students
practiced the painter's major scales
rounded their serious apples
placed light
saw colors in the colors
dappled jugs with mottled texture
again again
sameness melting
in the soft warmth of attention
showing deeper deeper
what is here
the glass the table the blank white wall

III. What We Are Given

Aphrodite Leaning on a Statue of Herself

I am not happy with the face—
too broad a smile, as if she doesn't understand
how serious the work. Her eyes, also, are wrong—
they're closed, she has an inward gaze—ridiculous.
Look, I have a job to do. Romance is hard enough.
Harmony among neighbors, fellow citizens
takes constant concentration on them all.

The work can be exhausting:
I allow myself diversion—
the bathing, the bejeweling,
nymphs attendant to each need.
This silly marble goddess would not see
the need for being frivolous:
to unbend from time to time
restores the heart.

Can you imagine how it is
to rest your elbow lightly
on someone's smooth idea of you?

Fascinators

The name alone would be enough,
but then the wisp of swooping
feather, snip of ribbon nesting
in the hair, winking with every
turn of head.

I first saw them early
on an April morning
when I was up to see
the televised royal wedding and,
alone with breakfast, watched
the fascinators.

And then I saw them everywhere—
in fashion magazines, in stores,
but lately not so much except
one check-out clerk at Whole Foods
wears a clutch of feathers
and a tiny veil as she snaps
a rubber band around the egg carton.

The Sacrament of Soup

This is what you do
when the call comes:
take the largest pot from the shelf
pour in water
chop and scrape
chop and scrape
carrots turnips
anything you have
any amount
add without measuring
lentils split peas marrow bone
anything you have
any amount.

Set it over fire.

This is what you do:
take the largest pot from the shelf
let your hands begin the work
let the fire begin the work
watch the incantation
of bubbles rising
again and again
fire
water
scrape
chop
anything you have
again and again.

This is all you can do.

looking across Somes Sound

the water all light and motion
wedge of shimmer
stripes of wind
ripples edging
tenderly to dulse and
Irish moss and rocks
smooth as the backs of whales

there is weight to the morning fog,
scent of fire
tree-dark hills
far-off sounds of loon and bells

shining children piling pinecones
beside the hammock
loud boat shattering far water
sharp wake cutting through shimmer
not to reach shore until
long after the boat has passed

The Way It Is Now

She calls with
good news and bad:
a baby on the way,
a friend in ICU.
I listen, tell her I am
glad and sad for her
as I am always now
for everyone.

Hotline

It isn't usually the jumpers—forget
what you might expect. The hard ones
come in the middle of the night or maybe
just about dinner time. That's when they
call, say I just wanted to talk
and then they tell you about
the apartment they never leave,
the street where everyone they knew
has moved away, the nursing home
where they live now. I'm trapped in here
with no one to talk to, they tell us.
Of course there are the ones who say
I saw your sign on the bridge,
and then you have to talk very
carefully, quietly, maybe
get a supervisor to listen, too. Steer
toward the pain, they told us in the training.
Don't tell them it will be okay—how can we
know that?—just be there. But that's not
most of them. Most of them, they're just
lonely. Some call every day, same time.
They say I took care of people all those years
and now there's no one to take care of me.
We can't stay on too long—twelve minutes, fourteen.
They understand. They say, "I know you have to go."

for LB and DB

One More Small Prayer of Healing

Like all who went before us
we bear the human burden—
flesh that crumbles, spirit that bends.
Comfort us as you comforted them,
be tender with us, wrap us in light:
teach us to praise our lives.

In the cell phone waiting lot

we arrive, each at our
own time, sit alone,
each in our own car,
wait. Then, summoned
by the call, we leave.
Another car arrives,
parks in our emptied place.

Likeness

Recipe for seeing:
thin silver on a copper sheet
buffed with powdered rouge
immersed in fumes of mercury
vapor of iodine, bromine
solution of salts

When he first saw daguerreotype,
subject and viewer visible together
in the mirror surface
visible together in a single frame
Frederick Douglass thought
he saw the end of hatred,
thought how no one
seeing eyes to eyes
and mouth to mouth
as if they spoke
could ever after be able
to deny kinship.

More Good News Than We Can Bear

It comes to us every day now:
one friend, after the stroke,
walks more steadily, tires less;
and the one whose brain surgery
was yesterday (for the spot missed
on the scan three months ago)
has pain only at 3 on a scale of one
to ten; another's in remission; and
the one whose care is "palliative"
had delicious soup for lunch. We
send them messages, stretch ourselves
to tell them what we're glad for.

Looking for Miracles

We are madly rifling through drawers
and closets, looking for the watch,
your cellphone (yes again),
the envelope with the unmailed check
and Mary stops her chores to mention
Saint Anthony.

Anthony, it seems, was schooled in loss.
Mary also, and though she's had it with religion,
tells us to ask him, "Come around
to find what's lost and can't be found"
and so we do, although we're not among his flock.

You don't believe in miracles
(and yet, oh, here—the watch was
on this shelf all the time)
though I do not scoff at
magic wands and crystals which—
who knows—*might* work
(the missing envelope had only
slipped beneath a magazine).

This Next Tenderness

The way he does it is
when the soap melts down to a sliver, he
pancakes it to the new bar—good and good,
more and more, like and like. And the way

she does it is
she drops the thin scrap onto the shower drain
to wash away, takes a fresh cake from the drawer,
weighs the heft and smoothness in her hand. That too,

she calls it cake, he calls it bar—vanilla/chocolate,
no right, no wrong, only an unhurried drift
as the passion to merge transforms into
a sanctity of differences, not black/white but

softer, maybe blue/green or shades of taupe
with borders opened out, enfolding both
builder of cairn and discarder of shard, marking
sacred ground for savoring of this, of that.

Stress Test

It is necessary to keep going
even as
it
gets
harder

No one will tell you
this continues
even after
monitoring
has
stopped

Each pairing its own universe

We're here to celebrate their years together
and they, with glasses raised, speak of
the work that is in marriage: hard,
hard work they say.

I picture toilers in the field,
heads down in solemn hoeing
of adjacent rows;
woodworkers at their common bench,

small tools arrayed around them,
sober focus on the task.
Why "work"? Why not,
instead something like tending,

like attention being paid?
Like gardening, with choose and
nurture, prune and weed where two
decide together, day by day,

what to encourage or toss aside?
Or like cooking—hearty loaf, gauzy souffle,
soup ingredients peeled and chopped,
simmer till flavors merge,

season to taste, correct the balance?
And if balance is the key, then why not
tightrope walkers, edging forward step by step,
the weight held lightly in their hands?

Open Letter (recipient undisclosed)

Why demand the drawn-out
farewell?
We would go quietly
if you asked. Just
tap us on the shoulder,
whisper, "time's up"
and we would take the cue.
We would go quietly.
Just ask.

We have always stood on water

though we believed it was ground.
We hardly noticed when the wet cold
reached our ankles, knees, but then saw how
it came higher, made us lift our chins
and breathe with slight anxiety, how some
who stood nearby went under early, fast,
as the waves continued without pause,
and how near where the flat earth drops off
the dragons wait, mouths open.

Only you

that's what we walked out to
after the ceremony
after we had walked in
to something sprightly by Schubert,
me in my new purple dress
and you in a grass green shirt,
after we had read the words we'd written
and the children had read the seven blessings
and we had drunk wine from a blue cup
and passed it around for everyone to have a sip
and we'd put on our new rings,
we walked down to the lake
while The Platters sang
only you can make the world seem bright,
only you can make the darkness light
and we all smiled because after darkness
we were lucky now in light.
It was my dream come true
and you were my one and only you.

What We Are Given

At first we held it between us
on our outstretched palms,
unbelieving and afraid
to let it move. We stared constantly,
held it to the light, its shine reflected
on our faces. It was too big to
close our hands around.
Then we began to trust its sturdiness,
let it roll onto our fingers, handled it
more casually, left fingermarks.
It grew familiar as our shoes,
an everyday companion, a pet.
We saw how easily we might
leave it lying on a table, let it roll
beneath a chair, gather dust,
saw how the art lies in more
than simply holding on.

*

Notes

"Good Day Sir or Madam" (p. 19) is a found poem, like many of its kind that appear frequently in inboxes.

"primitive" (p. 56) refers to the sculpture Bison Se Lechant (the Licking Bison), an outstanding example of paleolithic art now housed in the National Museum of Prehistory, Les Eyzies-de-Tayac, France. Dated approximately 14,000 B.C.E, the bison is carved in antler, sometimes referred to as "reindeer wood."

"Havdalah (Before You Leave)" (p. 60): Havdalah, in Jewish tradition, marks the end of the Sabbath and its separation from the other days of the week.

"Inventing Abstraction" (p. 62) grew out of a visit to a Museum of Modern Art exhibit of the same title, which explores how abstract art was created by artists throughout the world, working independently or under each others' influence beginning in 1911.

Acknowledgments

With thanks to:

the following publications where some of these poems first appeared: *Antiphon, The Common, Common Ground Review, Innisfree Poetry Journal, Lilith, A Mighty Room: a collection of poems written in Emily Dickinson's bedroom, Muddy River Poetry Review, Roanoke Review,* and *Solstice Literary Magazine;*

the Virginia Center for the Creative Arts, Every Other Thursday poets, The Breakfast Club, and Sisters in Art;

friends and family members who have offered gifts of connection and support;

and poets past and present whose work sustains and inspires me.

Ellen Steinbaum is the author of three previous poetry collections and a one-person play. An award-winning journalist and former *Boston Globe* columnist, she writes a blog, "Reading and Writing and the Occasional Recipe" which can be found at her web site, ellensteinbaum.com. She is originally from Wilmington, Delaware and now lives in Boston.